Banana Smoothie

Ingredients:

- 2 Bananas
- 120g of Vanilla Yogurt
- 120ml of Milk
- 2 tsp. of Honey
- Dash of Cinnamon
- 220g of Ice

Directions:

1. *Blend the ice.*
2. Blend all of the ingredients into the ice.

Nutritional Information:

- Calories: 223
- Total Fat: 1g
- Saturated Fat: 0g
- Carbohydrates: 24g
- Protein: 6g

Banana and Strawberry Smoothie

Ingredients:

- 1 Banana
- 200g of Strawberries
- 120g of Vanilla Yogurt
- 120ml of Milk
- 2 tsp. of honey
- Dash of Cinnamon
- 220g of Ice

Directions

1. *Blend the ice in a blender or food processor.*
2. Blend in the rest of the ingredients.

Nutritional Information:

- Calories: 235
- Total Fat: 2g
- Saturated Fat: 0g
- Carbohydrates: 21g
- Protein: 6.5g

Strawberry Shortcake Smoothie

Ingredients:

- 400g of Strawberries
- 150g of Pound Cake – Crumbled
- 320ml of Milk
- 400g of Ice
- 1 tsp. of Sweetener
- Topping – Whipped Cream
- Topping – Chopped Strawberries

Directions:

1. *Blend the ice.*
2. Add in the milk, sweetener, cake, and strawberries.
3. Top it with chopped strawberries and whipped cream.

Nutritional Information:

- Calories: 274
- Total Fat: 4g
- Saturated Fat: 0g
- Carbohydrates: 21g
- Protein: 7g

Triple Blended Berry Smoothie

Ingredients:

- 40g of Blackberries
- 65g of Strawberries
- 40g of Raspberries
- 220g of Ice
- 250ml of Milk
- 1 tsp. of Sweetener

Directions:

1. *Blend the ice.*
2. *Blend in the rest of the ingredients.*

Nutritional Information:

- Calories: 215
- Total Fat: 1g
- Saturated Fat: 0g
- Carbohydrates: 20g
- Protein: 5g

Orange Raspberry Smoothie

Ingredients:

- 250ml of Orange Juice
- 125g of Raspberries
- 125g of Plain Yogurt
- 220g of Ice
- 1 tsp. of Sweetener

Directions:

1. *Blend the ice.*
2. Blend the rest of the ingredients together.

Nutritional Information:

- Calories: 212
- Total Fat: 1g
- Saturated Fat: 0g
- Carbohydrates: 19g
- Protein: 4g

Mango Peach Banana Smoothie

Ingredients:

- 225g of Peaches – Fresh or Frozen
- 175g of Mango – Fresh or Frozen
- 250g of Plain Yogurt
- 220g of Ice
- ½ Banana
- 1 tsp. of Sweetener

Directions:

1. *Blend in the ice.*
2. Add in the rest of the ingredients and blend them together.

Nutritional Information:

- Calories: 210
- Total Fat: 1g
- Saturated Fat: 0g
- Carbohydrates: 18g
- Protein: 4g

Almond Honeydew Smoothie

Ingredients:

- 340 of Honeydew Melon – Chopped
- 250g of Almond Milk
- 220g of Ice
- 2 tsp. of Honey

Directions:

1. *Blend in the ice and the milk.*
2. Blend in the rest of the ingredients.

Nutritional Information:

- Calories: 178
- Total Fat: 1g
- Saturated Fat: 0g
- Carbohydrates: 17g
- Protein: 4g

Cantaloupe Smoothie

Ingredients:

- 320g of Cantaloupe – Chopped
- Juice from ½ Lime
- 3 Tbsp. of Sweetener
- 130ml of Water
- 220g of Ice

Directions:

1. *Blend the ice.*
2. Blend in the rest of the ingredients.

Nutritional Information:

- Calories: 157
- Total Fat: 1g
- Saturated Fat: 0g
- Carbohydrates: 18g
- Protein: 5g

Apple and Carrots Smoothie

Ingredients:

- 250ml of Carrot Juice
- 250ml of Apple Juice
- 420g of Ice

Directions:

- *Blend all of the ingredients together.*

Nutritional Information:

- Calories: 124
- Total Fat: 1g
- Saturated Fat: 0g
- Carbohydrates: 16g
- Protein: 3g

Spa Cucumber Smoothie

Ingredients:

- 2 Medium Cucumbers
- Juice from 1 Lime
- 120ml of Water
- 220g of Ice
- 3-4 Tbsp. of Honey

Directions:

1. Blend the ice and the water.
2. Blend in the rest of the ingredients.

Nutritional Information:

- Calories: 123
- Total Fat: 0g
- Saturated Fat: 0g
- Carbohydrates: 16g
- Protein: 3g

Cherry Vanilla Smoothie

Ingredients:

- 150g of Cherries – Frozen
- 300ml of Milk
- 3 Tbsp. of Sweetener
- ½ tsp. of Vanilla
- ¼ tsp. of Almond Extract
- Dash of Salt
- 220g of Ice

Directions:

1. *Blend the ice, salt, and milk.*
2. Blend in the rest of the ingredients.

Nutritional Information:

- Calories: 174
- Total Fat: 1g
- Saturated Fat: 0g
- Carbohydrates: 17g
- Protein: 4g

Grapefruit Smoothie

Ingredients:

- 2 Grapefruits
- 3-4 Tbsp. of Sweetener
- 220g of Ice
- Dash of Cinnamon

Directions:

1. Blend the ice.
2. Add in the sweetener.
3. Add in the grapefruits.
4. Dash the top with cinnamon.

Nutritional Information:

- Calories: 113
- Total Fat: 0g
- Saturated Fat: 0g
- Carbohydrates: 4g
- Protein: 21g

Ginger Banana Smoothie

Ingredients:

- 1 Banana
- 190g of Vanilla Yogurt
- 1 Tbsp. of Honey
- ½ tsp. of Ginger – Grated

Directions:

1. *Blend all of the ingredients together.*

Nutritional Information:

- Calories: 157
- Total Fat: 1g
- Saturated Fat: 0g
- Carbohydrates: 34g
- Protein: 5g

Mango Shake

Ingredients:

- 250g of Plain Yogurt
- 220g of Ice
- 1 Large Mango – Peeled, Pitted, Chopped
- 1 Tbsp. of Sweetener
- Mint Leaf

Directions:

1. Put all of the ingredients, except for the mint, into your blender.
2. Blend it until it is blend.
3. Garnish is with the mint.

Nutritional Information:

- Calories: 178
- Total Fat: 2g
- Saturated Fat: 0g
- Carbohydrates: 21g
- Protein: 4g

Blue Raspberry Shake

Ingredients:

- 200g of Blueberries – Frozen
- 125g of Raspberries – Frozen
- 4-5 Tbsp. of Plain Yogurt
- 250ml Water
- 3 Tbsp. of Sweetener

Directions:

1. *Put in the berries and the yogurt, then blend.*
2. *Blend in the rest of the ingredients.*

Nutritional Information:

- Calories: 189
- Total Fat: 2g
- Saturated Fat: 0g
- Carbohydrates: 24g
- Protein: 7g

Mixed Berry Shake

Ingredients:

- 400g of Strawberries – Washed, Hulled
- 120ml of Cranberry Juice Cocktail
- 2 Tbsp. of Sweetener
- 1 Pint of Strawberry Yogurt – Frozen

Directions:

1. *Combine all of the ingredients.*
2. *Garnish it with mint leaves.*

Nutritional Information:

- Calories: 230
- Total Fat: 3g
- Saturated Fat: 1g
- Carbohydrates: 25g
- Protein: 7g

Buttermilk Strawberry Shake

Ingredients:

- 300g of Strawberries – Frozen
- 600g of Buttermilk – Low Fat
- ½ tsp. of Vanilla Extract
- 2 Tbsp. of Sweetener

Directions:

1. *Place all of the ingredients in the blender.*
2. *Process them all until it is smooth.*

Nutritional Information:

- Calories: 254
- Total Fat: 2g
- Saturated Fat: 0g
- Carbohydrates: 27g
- Protein: 9g

Mixed Berry Shake

Ingredients:

- 1liter Vanilla Ice Cream – Sugar Free
- 180g of Berries – Unsweetened, Frozen
- 500ml of Milk – Almond

Directions:

1. Combine the sugar free ice cream, milk, and the berries.
2. Blend them until they are smooth.

Nutritional Information:

- Calories: 298
- Total Fat: 3g
- Saturated Fat: 0g
- Carbohydrates: 34g
- Protein: 8g

Cranberry Green Tea Shake

Ingredients:

- 60g of Cranberries – Frozen
- 75g of Blueberries – Frozen
- 5 Strawberries – Frozen
- 1 Banana
- 120ml of Green Tea – Cooled (Room Temperature)
- 60ml of Soy Milk
- 2 Tbsp. of Honey

Directions:

1. *Blend all of the ingredients together.*
2. *Drink immediately after.*

Nutritional Information:

- Calories: 157
- Total Fat: 1g
- Saturated Fat: 0g
- Carbohydrates: 34g
- Protein: 5g

The Energy Shake

Ingredients:

- 120ml of Orange Juice
- 4-5 Strawberries – Hulled, Sliced
- ½ Banana
- 70g of Silken Tofu
- 1 Tbsp. of Honey
- 6 Cubes of Ice

Directions:

1. *Blend the ice and the tofu.*
2. *Blend in the rest of the ingredients.*

Nutritional Information:

- Calories: 156
- Total Fat: 0g
- Saturated Fat: 0g
- Carbohydrates: 21g
- Protein: 4g

Yogurt and Fruit Shake

Ingredients:

- 100g of Cherries – Frozen
- 250g of Yogurt – Plain
- 250ml of Pomegranate Cherry Juice
- 1 Can (about 250g) of Pineapple – Crushed, Keep the Juice
- 1 Banana – Peeled, Sliced

Directions:

1. *Blend the ingredients together. Except for the banana slices.*
2. *Add the bananas to the top.*

Nutritional Information:

- Calories: 215
- Total Fat: 2g
- Saturated Fat: 0g
- Carbohydrates: 21g
- Protein: 7g

Mango Blackberry Shake

Ingredients:

- 270g of Blackberries – Frozen
- 165g of Mango Slices
- 250g of Tofu – Low Fat
- 250ml of Orange Juice
- 3 Tbsp. of Honey

Directions:

1. *Blend all of the ingredients together.*

Nutritional Information:

- Calories: 211
- Total Fat: 2g
- Saturated Fat: 0g
- Carbohydrates: 21g
- Protein: 4g

Strawberry Milk Shake

Ingredients:

- 240g of Strawberries – Stemmed, Sliced
- ½ tsp. of Vanilla Extract
- 450ml of Sugar Free Vanilla Ice Cream
- 60ml of Milk

Directions:

1. *Add in all of the ingredients.*

Nutritional Information:

- Calories: 213
- Total Fat: 2g
- Saturated Fat: 0g
- Carbohydrates: 22g
- Protein: 6g

Fruit Yogurt Shake

Ingredients:

- 350g of Sugar Free Vanilla Ice Cream
- 240g of Yogurt – Low Fat, Plain
- 130ml of Pineapple Orange Juice Concentrate – Thawed
- 400g of Strawberries – Frozen
- 1 Banana – Chopped

Directions:

1. *Blend in all of the ingredients.*
2. *Drink right after blending.*

Nutritional Information:

- Calories: 215
- Total Fat: 1g
- Saturated Fat: 0g
- Carbohydrates: 24g
- Protein: 6g

Choco Cherry Smoothie

Ingredients:

- 4 tbsp cocoa powder, unsweetened
- 200g cherries
- 500ml almond milk, unsweetened
- 2 tbsp chia seeds
- 45g rolled oats
- 2 dates

Directions:

1. *Add all ingredients into the blender and blend until smooth and creamy.*

Nutritional Value (Amount per Serving):

- Calories 748
- Fat 60.7 g
- Carbohydrates 56.4 g
- Sugar 27.6 g
- Protein 11.8 g

Melon Mint Smoothie

Ingredients:

- 500g ripe honeydew melon
- 440g ice
- 20 mint leaves
- 5 tbsp lemon juice
- 320g plain vegan yogurt

Directions:

1. Add all ingredients into the blender and blend until smooth and creamy.
2. Serve and enjoy.

Nutritional Value (Amount per Serving):

- Calories 249
- Fat 2.7 g
- Carbohydrates 44.1 g
- Sugar 41.6 g
- Protein 11.0 g

Zinger Ginger Honeydew Smoothie

Ingredients:

- 170g honeydew melon
- 1 inch/2cm ginger
- 1 ripe banana
- 150g watermelon
- 160g cantaloupe
- 250ml almond milk

Directions:

1. *Add all ingredients into the blender and blend until smooth.*

Nutritional Value (Amount per Serving):

- Calories 408
- Fat 29.2 g
- Carbohydrates 39.9 g
- Sugar 28.9 g
- Protein 5.0 g

Guava Smoothie

Ingredients:

- 1 guava, sliced
- 4 tbsp coconut milk
- 125g fresh raspberries
- 180g pomegranate seeds
- 60g ice cubes

Directions:

1. Add all ingredients into the blender and blend until smooth.
2. Serve immediately and enjoy.

Nutritional Value (Amount per Serving):

- Calories 132
- Fat 8.0 g
- Carbohydrates 15.4 g
- Sugar 7.7 g
- Protein 2.6 g

Cranberry Banana Smoothie

Ingredients:

- 120g cranberries
- 1 banana
- 1 orange
- 250ml almond milk, unsweetened
- 6 ice cubes

Directions:

1. *Add all ingredients into the blender and blend until smooth and creamy.*

Nutritional Value (Amount per Serving):

- Calories 402
- Fat 28.9 g
- Carbohydrates 35.9 g
- Sugar 21.8 g
- Protein 4.2 g

Apricot Berries Smoothie

Ingredients:

- 2 apricots, pitted
- 250ml almond milk
- 175g mix berries
- 220g ice cubes

Directions:

1. *Add all ingredients into the blender and blend until smooth and creamy.*
2. *Serve immediately and enjoy.*

Nutritional Value (Amount per Serving):

- Calories 365
- Fat 29.1 g
- Carbohydrates 27.6 g
- Sugar 20.8 g
- Protein 3.7 g

Pear Blueberry Smoothie

Ingredients:

- 200g blueberries
- 120ml water
- 1 pear, seeded and diced
- 400g plain vegan yogurt

Directions:

1. *Add all ingredients into the blender and blend until smooth.*

Nutritional Value (Amount per Serving):

- Calories 143
- Fat 1.4 g
- Carbohydrates 26.6 g
- Sugar 21.4 g
- Protein 5.9 g

Celery Cucumber Smoothie

Ingredients:

- 3 celery ribs
- 1 inch/2cm ginger
- Juice of a lemon
- 2 medium cucumbers

Directions:

1. *Add all ingredients into the blender and blend until smooth.*
2. *Serve chilled and enjoy.*

Nutritional Value (Amount per Serving):

- Calories 90
- Fat 0.7 g
- Carbohydrates 21.9 g
- Sugar 10.1 g
- Protein 3.9 g

Carrot Celery Ginger Smoothie

Ingredients:

- 2 medium carrots
- 4 celery sticks
- 1 inch/2cm ginger piece
- 1 lemon (juice)
- 3 green apples

Directions:

1. *Add all ingredients into the blender and blend until smooth.*
2. *Serve immediately and enjoy.*

Nutritional Value (Amount per Serving):

- Calories 199
- Fat 0.6 g
- Carbohydrates 52.2 g
- Sugar 37.8 g
- Protein 1.4 g

Turmeric Pineapple Smoothie

Ingredients:

- 1 inch/2cm fresh turmeric piece, peeled
- 225g pineapple, cut into pieces
- 1 tsp vanilla extract
- 250ml almond milk
- 1 banana
- 1 inch/2cm fresh ginger piece, peeled

Directions:

1. *Add banana, ginger, pineapple and turmeric in blender and blend until smooth.*
2. *Now add vanilla extract and almond milk and blend again until smooth and creamy.*
3. *Serve immediately and enjoy.*

Nutritional Value (Amount per Serving):

- Calories 376
- Fat 28.9 g
- Carbohydrates 31.2 g
- Sugar 19.6 g
- Protein 3.8 g

Cucumber Pineapple Grapefruit Smoothie

Ingredients:

- 1 cucumber
- 225g pineapple chunks
- 1 grapefruit
- 1 inch/2cm ginger piece

Directions:

1. *Add all ingredients into the blender and blend until smooth.*

Nutritional Value (Amount per Serving):

- Calories 84
- Fat 0.3 g
- Carbohydrates 21.5 g
- Sugar 15.1 g
- Protein 1.8 g

Turmeric Pumpkin Smoothie

Ingredients:

- 220g pumpkin
- 1 inch/2cm fresh turmeric piece
- 2 carrots, peeled
- 2 green apples
- 1/4 tsp cinnamon powder

Directions:

1. *Add all ingredients into the blender and blend until smooth.*

Nutritional Value (Amount per Serving):

- Calories 183
- Fat 0.7 g
- Carbohydrates 46.7 g
- Sugar 30.2 g
- Protein 2.5 g

Sweet Potato Ginger Smoothie

Ingredients:

- 1 sweet potato
- 1 inch/2cm fresh ginger
- 2 carrots
- 115g pineapple chunks

Directions:

1. *Add all ingredients into the blender and blend until smooth.*

Nutritional Value (Amount per Serving):

- Calories 97
- Fat 0.3 g
- Carbohydrates 23.2 g
- Sugar 10.8 g
- Protein 1.9 g

Cucumber Ginger Smoothie

Ingredients:

- 1/2 fennel
- 1 large cucumber
- 1 inch/2cm fresh ginger
- 1/4 lemon (juice)
- 2 green apples
- 4 celery ribs

Directions:

1. *Add all ingredients into the blender and blend until smooth.*

Nutritional Value (Amount per Serving):

- Calories 139
- Fat 0.6 g
- Carbohydrates 36.3 g
- Sugar 25.7 g
- Protein 1.6 g

Apple Peanut Butter Smoothie

Ingredients:

- 2 medium apples, diced
- 2 tbsp peanut butter
- 440g ice cubes
- 1 tsp cinnamon

Directions:

1. Add apple, peanut butter and ice cubes into the blender and blend until smooth and creamy.
2. Pour into the glasses and sprinkle with cinnamon on top.

Nutritional Value (Amount per Serving):

- Calories 106
- Fat 4.2 g
- Carbohydrates 17.4 g
- Sugar 12.4 g
- Protein 2.3 g

Chocolate Avocado Smoothie

Ingredients:

- 1/2 avocado, remove seed and scoop out
- 2 tbsp cocoa powder
- 320ml almond milk, unsweetened
- 3 tbsp peanut butter
- 1 medium ripe banana

Directions:

1. *Add all ingredients into the blender and blend until smooth and creamy.*

Nutritional Value (Amount per Serving):

- Calories 738
- Fat 65.7 g
- Carbohydrates 39.8 g
- Sugar 20.1 g
- Protein 12.7 g

Image sources/Printing information

Pictures cover: depositphotos. com;

@ ehaurylik; @ derepente; @Anna_Shepulova

Print edition black and white paperback:

Amazon Media EU S.à.r.l.

5 Rue Plaetis

L-2338 Luxembourg

Other printouts:

epubli, a service of neopubli GmbH, Berlin

Publisher:

BookRix GmbH & Co. KG

Sonnenstraße 23

80331 München

Deutschland

Printed in Great Britain
by Amazon

83252595R00027